Twigs for the Nest

Priscilla Mileski

BookLeaf
Publishing

India | USA | UK

Presentation by *BookLeaf Publishing*

Web: www.bookleafpub.com

E-mail: info@bookleafpub.com

ISBN: 9789360948085

First edition 2024

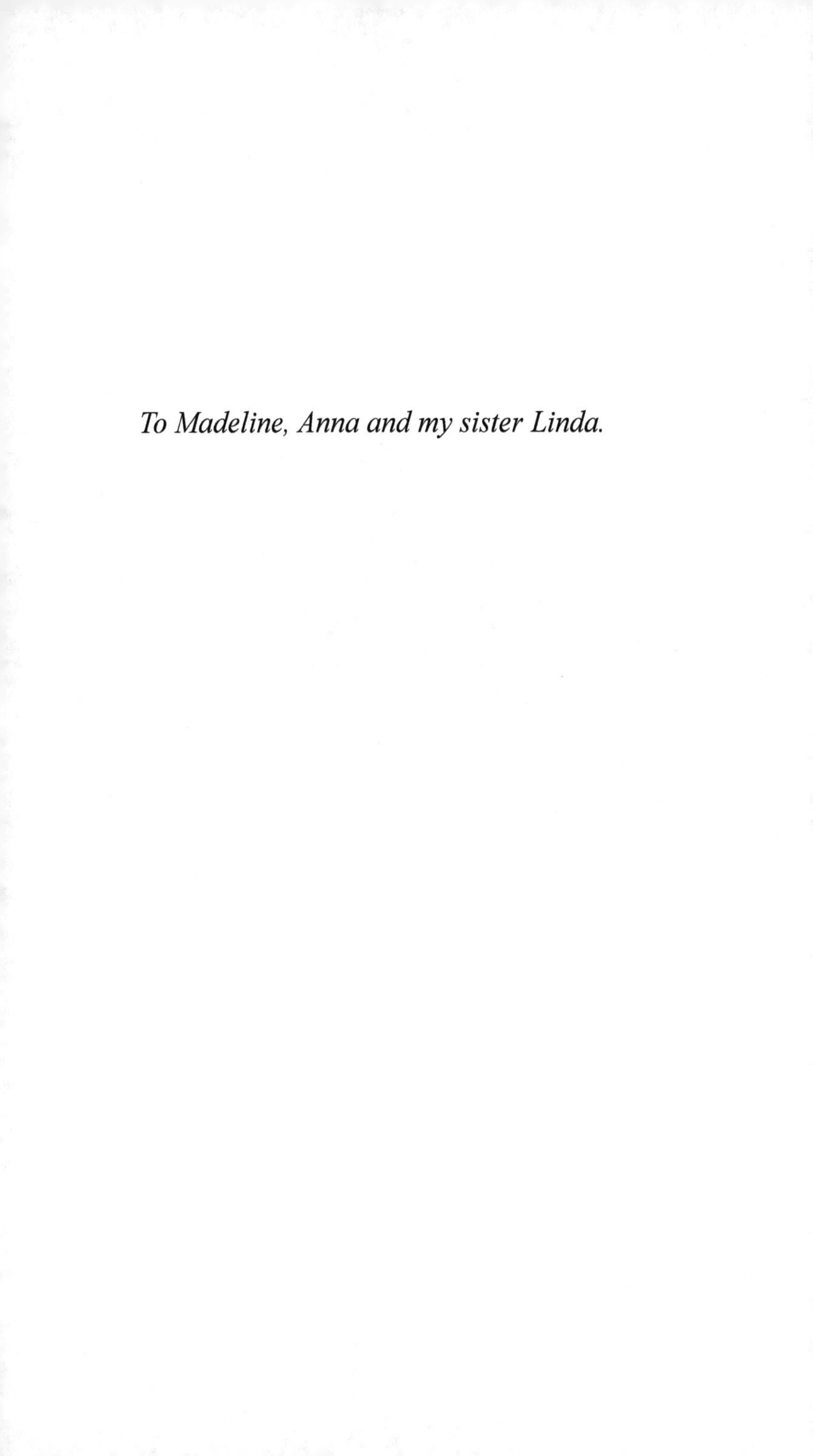

PREFACE

Everyday the birds I observe tell a story that I want to remember. Those brief moments are best captured in a short poem. They lift my spirit and encourage me to be quiet and watch. Enjoy the birds you encounter.

Flicker

A Northern flicker
nothing but a scatter
of feathers, not a bone in sight.

Each shaft a streak of gold.
His downy feathers soft beige
with sharp, dark marks.

Did you ever imagine
the mason jar on my desk
would hold your legacy?

House Sparrow

The old wooden swing
needs a new coat of paint.
But still, it swings nicely.

The green table
beside me holds a tray of seed
and the birds come.

House sparrow
lands in the dogwood.
He watches me watch him.

He comes to feed so close to me
I can feel his hunger.
My day, my year is changed.

Hawk

The hawk is back
stalking the small
aviary birds
in my backyard.

We only see him
in the winter, in the cold.
He prefers hunting the fields
outside of town.

I hear him sigh to his hawk mate.

There is no joy in hunting
when humans
protect the prey.

Winter Birds

Little winter birds
scurry and squabble
over offerings of winter seed.
Corn, suet, millet.
The water soon will freeze.

Empty sunflower hulls
litter mud and hay.
When the thaw comes
they will be raked,
feeders given new ground.

All I need to do is watch.
And offer.
It is all I can do.

Finch

Little finch
building your nest
feathers and string.

Two white eggs
a wobbly head
bald little babe.

Tender finch
tending the young
feathers and string.

Feeding the Birds

Winter birds so easily enticed,
you've stayed and I must feed
for what for me is simply joy
for you is deadly need.

Bob the Pigeon

Struts his stuff,
murmurs to himself.
He shuns the budgies,
those pirates of green
and blue iridescence.

Catbird Watches Me

With a black cap
and a dapper gray coat
he hops limb to limb,
shrub to shrub.

His tail flicks from
side to side and
he eyes my every move.
Mew! Mew!

Three years they've nested
just outside the door.
I put out sweet, soft raisins,
a special treat.

On my evening walk they follow
just a bit. They flit tree to tree
wagging their tails
and scolding me.

Mew! Mew!

Little Grackle Fledgling

Little grackle fledgling
hops each step
close behind his mother.
Crisscrossing the lawn,
she ignores him
as she stabs at bugs,

Still in his fluffy gray down,
he flutters frantically
and nips her tail feathers to complain.

Pelicans on Big Assawoman Bay

Once, sitting on a sand dune
looking east at the Atlantic,
I saw a formation of pelicans headed west
to the inland waters of the Bay.

A hum of bombers on a raid
or leftover pterodactyls,
they race the sunset, skim
the calm waters and come to a flapping rest.

Catbird and Robin

A robin jumps in to snag an insect
from catbird who is at the base of the tree.
They get into a noisy tussle,
wings beat against wings
with a flurry of forays.

Suddenly robin take two steps back
then flits to the next yard.
It's a small defeat where
so many bugs abound.
Catbird throws back his head to gulp his meal.

Cacophony

Grackle and starling
grackle, grackle, grackle
calling and poking the ground.
Stealing all the sparrow's seed,
upsetting the feeder,
pouring the spill to their cohorts.

The cacophony of starling
and grackle calling in the Fall.

Budgerigars

Twelve of them
gossip all day, forage
for spilled seed, preen
to the tips of their pencil-long tails.

Sometimes they sing facing the wall,
amplifying their own snappy chatter.

Occasionally there is a spat,
the indignation of a favored perch
commandeered,
but it ends quickly as there is much
to much to discuss in the little backyard aviary.

Whoosh!

The sound of a thousand
blackbirds lifting
from the trees in a
bramble-edged clearing
in the stillness of the wood.

They rise to the skies
wave after wave, inking
the clear blue February dome.
They shout their return over
and over to the forest and the field.

Where Owl?

Sitting on the porch
I hear a mob of crows, seven or eight
loud and persistent.

I slow-walk across the street
to check the trees,
there might be an owl.

The man in his car on his phone
might wonder why this old woman
stares into the trees.

Just listening to the hear
what the birds tell me.

It's not easy spotting owls
in the still green leaves.

The Aviary

In the little backyard aviary,
the Happy Lady Aviary
on Happy Lady Lane
I am, in fact,
Happy.

Sandpipers

My day trip to the ocean
is made complete
by the scurrying little feet
of the sandpipers.

It is mid-winter,
there are only four,
but enough to balance the hovering
boisterous flock of seagulls.

White Pigeon

Bob comes outside
to inspect the white
world of snow.
A whorl of feather-light
flakes swirl around and
into the aviary.

He takes to the highest shelf,
puffs himself and struts in
tight circles of pigeon pout.

Then he stops, fans his tail feathers
in a spread of clean
white brilliance.

This is his kingdom.

Checking the Bluebird Boxes

This year all six bluebird boxes
have nests, one tree swallow
three bluebird
and two chickadee.

The tiny black-capped
chickadee builds
layer upon layer of twig, grass
and soft green moss.

Five little brown-speckled eggs
rest patient and quiet.

Blue Jay

Blue jay yells
for me to bring his peanuts
and fusses at me to hurry
as I fill the feeders.

Then, in his best hawk voice,
shouts an alarm
piercing the morning
to scare the sparrows to the hedge.

He snags the best peanut,
stuffs another in his cheek.
His bully ways forgiven
for the brash flash of blue.

Cardinals

Two pair of cardinals
will nest again in the yard
but not before an extended
game of love chase and seek.

They call and respond
a red cardinal song
specific, imperative
and valentine sweet.